ZERO TAXES IN CYPRUS

MOVE TO THE SUN AND LOWER YOUR TAXES

FREEDOM & BUSINESS SERIES

ALEX ABOVE

Copyright © 2024 by ALEX ABOVE

All rights reserved.

No part of this book may be reproduced in any form or by any electronic or mechanical means, including information storage and retrieval systems, without written permission from the author, except for the use of brief quotations in a book review.

The information provided in this book is for informational purposes only and is not intended as legal, financial or tax advice. Although every effort has been made to ensure the accuracy and completeness of the contents, tax laws and regulations are subject to change and their application may vary according to individual circumstances.

Readers are advised to consult qualified professionals, such as tax advisers, accountants or legal experts, before making any decisions based on the information presented in this book. The author and publisher disclaim any liability for any loss or damage incurred by any person or entity relying on the information in this book.

This book does not establish any form of professional relationship between the reader and the author or publisher. The content should not be used as a substitute for professional advice and counseling specific to your situation.

FOREWORD

In an increasingly globalized world, where the freedom to choose where to live and work is accompanied by the complexity of international tax systems, Cyprus stands out as a beacon for individuals and businesses seeking tax efficiency.

"(Almost) Zero Taxes in Cyprus" offers a deep dive into one of Europe's most interesting tax jurisdictions. This book is an essential guide to understanding how Cyprus' favorable tax laws, particularly its non-dom regime, can help you maximize your savings, protect your wealth, and strategically position your business for growth.

Whether you are an expatriate, entrepreneur or business executive, this guide will enable you to navigate the Cypriot tax landscape with confidence and take full advantage of its tax benefits.

In addition to the financial benefits, Cyprus offers an exceptional lifestyle that perfectly complements the tax benefits. Imagine living in a Mediterranean paradise where over 300 days of sunshine accompany you all year round and pristine beaches are just minutes away. Cyprus is not just a tax haven, it is a paradise for life. The island boasts a rich cultural heritage, vibrant communities and a high standard of living, all while maintaining a relatively low cost of living compared to other European countries.

Cyprus offers a balanced and fulfilling lifestyle that makes it more than a smart financial move-it is a move toward a better quality of life.

Aerial view of a beach in Cyprus

CHAPTER 1
INTRODUCTION TO THE CYPRUS TAXATION SYSTEM

OVERVIEW OF THE CYPRUS TAX SYSTEM

Cyprus boasts a highly attractive and efficient tax system, making it a prime destination for individuals and companies seeking favorable tax treatment. The cornerstone of the Cyprus tax system is its corporate tax rate, which stands at 12.5%, one of the lowest in the European Union (lower than Cyprus are Montenegro and Hungary at 9 percent and Bulgaria at 10 percent where there are; however, dividend taxes that are absent in Cyprus' non-dom regime). This competitive rate is complemented by a range of exemptions, allowances, and deductions that enhance the appeal of Cyprus as a business hub.

Cyprus operates on a worldwide income tax system, meaning that residents of Cyprus are taxed on their worldwide income, not just income sourced from Cyprus. However, under the non-domicile (non-dom) regime, specific exemptions apply to certain types of foreign-sourced income, such as dividends and interest.

In addition to the low corporate tax rate, Cyprus provides various other tax benefits. These include exemptions on dividend income, no capital gains tax on the disposal of securities, and an extensive network of double taxation treaties with over 60 countries. These treaties help eliminate double taxation and can reduce withholding taxes on dividends, interest, and royalties, further enhancing the tax efficiency of operating in Cyprus.

Value Added Tax (VAT) in Cyprus is set at a standard rate of 19%, with reduced rates of 9% and 5% applicable to certain goods and services and some items being completely exempt. VAT compliance is straightforward, with the VAT Department offering electronic submission of returns and payments, simplifying the process for businesses. Intra-community transactions between VAT numbers registered in VIES can take advantage of the reverse-charge mechanism, and thus, it is possible to issue invoices without VAT to foreign entities.

Cyprus adheres to the One Stop Shop (OSS) system for goods to simplify VAT transactions. In addition, for those who need to carry out product imports and store goods in other EU countries, it is always possible to place the Cyprus VAT registration alongside the VAT and EORI numbers (Economic Operators Registration and Identification) of other member countries.

Personal income tax in Cyprus is progressive, with rates ranging from 0% to 35%. Individuals earning up to €19,500 per year are exempt from income tax, while higher earners are taxed at increasing rates. The personal tax system includes various allowances and deductions, such as contributions to social insurance, pension funds, and other approved funds, which can reduce taxable income.

BENEFITS OF CYPRUS AS A TAX JURISDICTION

The low rate and various exemptions and deductions provide substantial tax savings for businesses. The strategic geographical location of Cyprus, at the crossroads of Europe, Asia, and Africa, further enhances its appeal. This position allows companies based in Cyprus to quickly access key markets across these regions. Additionally, Cyprus is a member of the European Union, which provides businesses access to the EU's single market and numerous trade agreements.

Cyprus's legal and regulatory framework is based on English Common Law principles, providing a familiar and reliable legal environment for international businesses. The country's legal system is transparent and efficient, ensuring businesses can confidently operate. Moreover, the government of Cyprus has shown a solid commitment to maintaining and enhancing a business-friendly environment through continuous improvements to legislation and administrative procedures.

Another key benefit is the highly skilled and multilingual workforce available in Cyprus. The education system in Cyprus produces graduates with high levels of expertise, particularly in finance, accounting, law, and IT. This talent pool, combined with the high standard of living and attractive climate, makes Cyprus an appealing destination for businesses and expatriates.

The Cyprus government offers various incentives to encourage foreign direct investment and establishing businesses on the island. These incentives include grants and subsidies for research and development, innovation, and technology projects. Additionally, the government has implemented a series of measures to streamline the process of setting up and operating a business in Cyprus, reducing administrative burdens and costs.

Cyprus's banking and financial services sector is well-developed and robust, offering various services to individuals and businesses. The

Central Bank of Cyprus regulates the industry and complies with international standards, ensuring high security and reliability for financial transactions. Numerous international banks and financial institutions further enhance Cyprus's appeal as a financial hub.

The quality of life in Cyprus is another important factor that attracts both businesses and individuals. The island offers a pleasant Mediterranean climate, beautiful landscapes, and a high standard of living. The cost of living in Cyprus is relatively low compared to other EU countries, and the healthcare and education systems are of high quality. These factors and the favorable tax regime make Cyprus an ideal location for expatriates and their families.

HISTORICAL CONTEXT AND EVOLUTION OF CYPRUS TAX LAWS

Cyprus gained independence from British rule in 1960, and the initial tax system was primarily inherited from the British colonial administration. The early years of independence saw the establishment of basic tax laws, including personal and corporate income taxes, designed to provide the necessary revenue for the newly independent state.

In the following decades, Cyprus embarked on a path of economic development, gradually transforming itself from an agrarian economy to a service-oriented one. The 1974 Turkish invasion and the subsequent island division profoundly impacted the economy, prompting the government to implement measures to attract foreign investment and stimulate economic growth.

One of the critical milestones in the evolution of Cyprus tax laws was the introduction of the Income Tax Law in 1961, which laid the foundation for the modern tax system. This law established the framework for personal and corporate income taxation, setting out the principles of tax residence, determining taxable income, and the applicable tax rates.

The 1980s and 1990s saw significant reforms to modernize the tax system and enhance its attractiveness to foreign investors. In 1981, the Special Contribution for the Defence of the Republic Law was introduced, which imposed a levy on interest, dividend, and rental income. This levy, known as the Special Defence Contribution (SDC), was designed to generate additional revenue for the state and support national defense efforts.

The 1990s also witnessed the Value Added Tax (VAT) introduction in 1992 in response to Cyprus's efforts to align with European Union standards and prepare for eventual EU membership. VAT replaced the previous system of indirect taxes and introduced a more transparent and efficient method of taxing goods and services.

Cyprus's accession to the European Union in 2004 marked a significant turning point in the evolution of its tax laws. Cyprus undertook extensive tax reforms to harmonize its tax system with EU directives and international standards as part of the accession process. These reforms included reducing the corporate tax rate to 10%, making it one of the lowest in the EU, and introducing anti-avoidance measures to prevent tax evasion and ensure compliance with EU rules.

The global financial crisis of 2008-2009 significantly impacted the island's economy, leading to a severe banking crisis in 2013. In response, the government implemented a series of austerity measures and tax reforms to stabilize the economy and restore investor confidence. These measures included increasing the corporate tax rate from 10% to 12.5%, introducing additional levies on financial institutions, and enhancing tax compliance and enforcement.

In recent years, Cyprus has refined and enhanced its tax system to maintain its competitiveness as a tax jurisdiction. The introduction of the non-domicile (non-dom) regime in 2015 was a significant development aimed at attracting high-net-worth individuals and expatriates by offering substantial tax exemptions on foreign-sourced income. This regime has proven to be highly successful, significantly boosting the appeal of Cyprus as a destination for expatriates and international investors.

The evolution of Cyprus tax laws has also been influenced by the country's commitment to international tax transparency and cooperation. Cyprus is a signatory to various international agreements, including the OECD's Common Reporting Standard (CRS) and the Base Erosion and Profit Shifting (BEPS) initiative. These agreements require Cyprus to exchange financial information with other jurisdictions and implement measures to combat tax evasion and aggressive tax planning.

The continuous reforms and improvements have positioned Cyprus as a competitive and reliable tax haven, offering substantial benefits to both individuals and businesses.

CHAPTER 2
UNDERSTANDING THE NON-DOM REGIME IN CYPRUS

DEFINITION AND CRITERIA

The concept of the non-domiciled (non-dom) regime is integral to understanding the tax landscape in Cyprus. The non-dom status in Cyprus is designed to attract high-net-worth individuals, digital nomads, and expatriates by offering significant tax benefits. **A non-dom individual in Cyprus is someone who, while being a resident for tax purposes, is not considered domiciled in Cyprus for tax purposes.**

To qualify for this status, an individual must meet specific residency requirements. The primary criterion is the "183-day rule," which stipulates that an individual must spend more than 183 days in Cyprus within a tax year to be considered a tax resident. Alternatively, the "60-day rule" can apply if the individual:

- Does not reside in another country for more than 183 days in a tax year.
- Is not a tax resident in any other country.
- Resides in Cyprus for at least 60 days in a tax year.
- Maintains a permanent residence in Cyprus, either owned or rented.

In addition to these residency criteria, an individual must not be domiciled in Cyprus. Generally, domicile is determined by the individual's origin, intention to reside permanently in a place, and personal circumstances. An individual is considered domiciled in Cyprus if they have been a resident for at least 17 out of the last 20 years. Those who were not may apply for non-dom status.

TAX ADVANTAGES OF THE NON-DOM REGIME

One of the most significant advantages is the exemption from the Special Defence Contribution (SDC). The SDC is typically imposed on dividends, interest, and rental income earned by Cyprus tax residents. However, **non-dom individuals are exempt from the SDC on foreign-sourced dividend and interest income, as well as on rental income from abroad**. This exemption can result in significant tax savings, particularly for those with substantial passive income streams or who work with online businesses.

Another key benefit is the exemption from capital gains tax on profits from the sale of securities, irrespective of whether these securities are based in Cyprus or abroad. This includes shares, bonds, debentures, and other financial instruments. The absence of capital gains tax on these transactions makes Cyprus an attractive jurisdiction for investors and those involved in international financial markets.

Non-dom individuals also benefit from favorable personal income tax rates. While Cyprus operates a progressive personal income tax system, with rates ranging from 0% to 35%, **non-doms can utilize various allowances and deductions to minimize their taxable income**. Additionally, foreign pension income can be taxed at a flat rate of 5%, with an annual exemption of €3,420, providing further tax efficiency for retirees.

The tax advantages of this regime extend to other areas, such as estate and inheritance planning: Cyprus does not impose inheritance or estate taxes, making it an appealing jurisdiction for individuals seeking to optimize their estate planning and ensure the efficient transfer of wealth to future generations.

Moreover, the non-dom regime in Cyprus includes provisions for tax credits and reliefs. Non-doms can claim a credit for foreign taxes paid on income sourced from abroad, preventing double taxation and ensuring that individuals do not face an excessive tax burden.

COMPARISON WITH OTHER NON-DOM REGIMES GLOBALLY

When comparing the non-dom regime in Cyprus with those of other countries, it becomes evident that Cyprus offers a highly competitive and advantageous system. Several countries, including the United Kingdom, Ireland, and Malta, have implemented non-dom regimes to attract expatriates and high-net-worth individuals. However, there are distinct differences in the criteria and benefits provided by each jurisdiction.

The United Kingdom, for example, has a long-established non-dom regime that allows individuals to be taxed on a remittance basis, meaning they are only taxed on foreign income and gains if they are remitted to the UK. However, this regime includes a remittance basis charge, which increases the longer an individual resides in the UK. For individuals who have been UK residents for seven out of the previous nine tax years, the charge is £30,000, rising to £60,000 for those who have been residents for 12 out of the previous 14 tax years. This charge can significantly reduce the attractiveness of the UK non-dom regime compared to Cyprus, where no such charge exists.

Ireland also offers a non-dom regime that taxes individuals on a remittance basis. However, the Irish regime is less favorable than Cyprus's regarding the breadth of income and gains exempted from tax. In Ireland, only foreign employment income is taxed on a remittance basis, while other foreign income and gains are subject to Irish tax. Additionally, the Irish regime does not provide the same level of dividend and interest income exemptions as Cyprus.

Malta's non-dom regime is more similar to Cyprus, offering a remittance basis of taxation for foreign income and gains. However, Malta imposes a minimum tax of €5,000 annually on foreign income, regardless of whether it is remitted to Malta. This minimum tax can be a deterrent for individuals with lower foreign income levels. Additionally, while Malta offers exemptions on certain types of income, it does not provide the same comprehensive exemptions on dividend and interest income as Cyprus.

SAVINGS FOR EXPATRIATES

To better understand the practical implications of the non-dom regime in Cyprus, consider the case of an expatriate individual relocating to Cyprus. Mr. Smith has significant investments in dividend-paying stocks, interest-earning bonds, and rental properties abroad. Under the Cyprus non-dom regime, Mr. Smith can enjoy the following benefits:

- **Dividend Income**: Dividends received from foreign stocks are fully exempt from taxation under the non-dom regime, providing Mr. Smith with substantial tax savings compared to jurisdictions that tax foreign dividends.
- **Interest Income**: Interest earned from foreign bonds is also exempt from the Special Defence Contribution, further reducing Mr. Smith's tax liability.
- **Rental Income**: Rental income from properties located outside Cyprus is not subject to the Special Defence Contribution, making it a highly tax-efficient source of income.
- **Capital Gains**: Any profits from the sale of foreign securities are exempt from capital gains tax, allowing Mr. Smith to reinvest his gains without additional taxes.

These exemptions can lead to significant tax savings, enhancing Mr. Smith's overall financial position and providing more capital for further investment or personal use.

Additionally, consider the case of a high-net-worth individual, Mrs. Johnson, who has decided to retire in Cyprus. Mrs. Johnson receives a substantial pension from her former employment abroad. Under the Cyprus non-dom regime, her foreign pension income can be taxed at a flat rate of 5%, with an annual exemption of €3,420. This low tax rate ensures that Mrs. Johnson retains more of her pension income compared to higher tax rates in other jurisdictions, providing her with greater financial security in retirement.

Finally, consider the case of Ricardo, a digital nomad originally from Germany. He has built a successful online business primarily focused on publishing eBooks through Amazon Kindle Direct Publishing (KDP). In addition to his Amazon KDP business, Ricardo generates income from affiliate marketing. As his business grew, Ricardo realized that he needed a more favorable tax regime to optimize his income and manage his growing business more efficiently:

- **Exemption from Taxes on Dividends and Interest:** Dividends received from his company are fully exempt from taxation. Ricardo would also be exempt from paying the Special Defence Contribution (SDC) on dividends and interest income.
- **Low Corporate Tax Rate:** Cyprus offers a corporate tax rate of 12.5%, one of the lowest in the EU. Ricardo could significantly reduce his business's overall tax burden by relocating his company to Cyprus.
- **No Tax on KDP Royalties:** As a Non-Dom resident, Ricardo's income from sources outside of Cyprus, such as his Amazon KDP royalties and affiliate marketing income, would not be subject to Cypriot taxation, provided the income is not remitted to Cyprus.

USEFUL TIPS FOR NON-DOM APPLICANTS

For individuals considering applying for non-dom status in Cyprus, several practical tips can help ensure a smooth and successful process:

- **Residency Planning**: Ensure compliance with the residency criteria by meticulously planning your days in Cyprus. Maintain accurate records of your travel dates and ensure that you meet the 183-day or 60-day rule requirements. I suggest the "Country Days Tracker" smartphone application, which automatically updates your presence in the various states and allows you to export a detailed list in Excel with the relevant

evidence (GPS location, location detected in photos taken) to show in case of audits.
- **Permanent Residence**: Secure a permanent residence in Cyprus, whether owned or rented (with at least a 12-month rental agreement), to satisfy the residency criteria and provide proof of your intention to reside in Cyprus.
- **Documentation**: Prepare and maintain all necessary documentation, including proof of foreign income sources, tax residency certificates from previous jurisdictions, and any other relevant records that may be required during the application process.
- **Professional Advice**: Seek advice from tax professionals or advisors specializing in Cyprus taxation. They can provide valuable insights, assist with the application process, and ensure compliance with all relevant tax laws and regulations.
- **Regular Reviews**: Regularly review your tax position and residency status to ensure continued compliance with the non-dom regime requirements. This proactive approach can help you avoid potential issues and optimize your tax liabilities.

By following these tips and understanding the comprehensive benefits of the Cyprus non-dom regime, individuals can effectively leverage the tax advantages offered by Cyprus and achieve substantial tax savings.

DEFINITION AND CRITERIA FOR NON-DOM STATUS

As we have seen above, to qualify for non-dom status in Cyprus, an individual must meet specific criteria related to residency and domicile. In legal terms, domicile refers to the country that a person treats as their permanent home or has a substantial connection with. There are two primary types of domicile: domicile of origin and domicile of choice. A domicile of origin is typically acquired at birth, based on the domicile of the individual's father. In contrast, a domicile of choice is acquired by establishing a new permanent home in a different country.

In Cyprus, the key criteria for obtaining non-dom status are based on the individual's residency status. To be considered a tax resident in Cyprus, an individual must meet one of the following conditions:

1. **183-Day Rule**: The individual must reside in Cyprus for at least 183 days within a tax year.
2. **60-Day Rule**: Introduced in 2017, this rule provides an alternative for individuals who do not meet the 183-day requirement. Under the 60-day rule, an individual can still be considered a tax resident in Cyprus if they:

- Do not reside in another country for more than 183 days within the same tax year.
- Do not hold tax residency in any other country.
- Reside in Cyprus for at least 60 days within the tax year.
- Maintain a permanent residence in Cyprus, either owned or rented.
- Carry on a business in Cyprus, be employed in Cyprus, or hold an office with a Cyprus tax-resident company.

It is important to note that even if an individual meets the residency requirements, they must also ensure they are not considered domiciled in Cyprus (not having been a tax resident of Cyprus for at least 17 of the last 20 years).

TAX BENEFITS IN DETAIL NON-DOM REGIME

Let's look at the main tax advantages of this scheme in detail.

Dividend Income

Under the non-dom regime, **dividend income received by non-domiciled individuals is exempt from SDC. This exemption applies to both domestic and foreign dividends**. This means that non-doms can receive dividends from their investments or business interests without being subject to the 17% SDC that would otherwise apply to such income.

Interest Income

Non-domiciled individuals are also **exempt from SDC on interest income, which includes interest earned on bank deposits, bonds, and other interest-bearing investments**. The standard SDC rate on interest income for domiciled individuals is 30%, but non-doms can benefit from a complete exemption to maximize their returns on interest-bearing assets.

Rental Income

Rental income received from abroad is another category of income that benefits from SDC exemption under the non-dom regime. Non-domiciled individuals can receive rental income from their properties outside Cyprus without being subject to the 3% SDC that applies to such income for domiciled individuals.

Capital Gains

In addition to the exemptions on dividend, interest, and rental income, non-domiciled individuals can also benefit from favorable treatment of capital gains. Cyprus does not impose capital gains tax on the disposal of securities, irrespective of whether the individual is domiciled or non-domiciled.

Foreign Pension Income

Foreign pension income received by non-domiciled individuals is also treated favorably under the Cyprus tax regime. Non-doms can choose to be taxed on their foreign pension income at a flat rate of 5% for amounts exceeding €3,420 annually, or they can opt for the standard progressive tax rates.

Other Benefits

Beyond the specific exemptions and favorable treatments mentioned above, non-domiciled individuals in Cyprus also benefit from the general advantages of the Cyprus tax system. These include the absence of wealth, inheritance, and gift taxes. Additionally, Cyprus offers a high personal tax-free threshold and various deductions and allowances that can further reduce taxable income.

GHS (GESY): A SMALL CONTRIBUTION ON DIVIDENDS

It should be noted that a small mandatory contribution is made in Cyprus to finance public health care. The GHS (General Healthcare System - commonly called GeSY) is a mandatory contribution in Cyprus that finances the national healthcare system. It applies to various forms of income, including salaries, pensions, and dividends. For dividends, **the contribution is typically 2.65%. This applies to all dividends received by residents of Cyprus, including Non-Dom residents**. The GHS contribution on dividends is capped annually. The maximum amount of dividend income subject to GHS contributions is €180,000. Therefore, the maximum contribution on dividends per individual is €4,770 (2.65% of €180,000).

APPLICATION PROCESS FOR NON-DOM STATUS

The application process for obtaining non-dom status in Cyprus is straightforward but requires careful documentation and adherence to procedural requirements. The process can be broadly outlined as follows:

- **Determining Eligibility**: The first step is to ascertain eligibility based on the criteria mentioned earlier. Individuals should evaluate their domicile status, tax residency, income sources, and intent to relocate to Cyprus.
- **Establishing Tax Residency**: To apply for non-dom status, individuals must first establish their tax residency in Cyprus. This involves spending the required number of days in the country (183 days or 60 days under the 60-day rule) and ensuring they do not meet tax residency criteria in any other country. Maintaining proper records of travel, accommodation, and local activities is crucial for this step.
- **Submitting an Application**: Once eligibility and tax residency are confirmed, individuals can apply to the Cyprus Tax Department. The application typically includes:
- A completed application form.
- Proof of tax residency, such as a residency certificate or tax registration.
- Documentation of domicile status, such as birth certificates or evidence of residence abroad.
- Evidence of economic ties to Cyprus includes employment contracts, business registrations, or property leases.
- **Review and Approval**: The Cyprus Tax Department reviews the application and supporting documents. The review process aims to verify that all eligibility criteria are met and that the individual genuinely intends to establish a presence in Cyprus. The department may request additional information or clarification during this stage.
- **Issuance of Non-Dom Status**: Upon approval, the individual is granted non-dom status, which is typically confirmed through an official letter or certificate. This status allows the individual to benefit from the tax exemptions and incentives associated with the non-dom regime.
- **Ongoing Compliance**: Maintaining non-dom status requires ongoing compliance with residency and income generation requirements. Individuals must continue to meet the tax residency criteria and ensure that their economic activities align with the conditions of the non-dom regime. The Cyprus

Tax Department may conduct regular reviews and audits to ensure compliance.

THE TAX ADVANTAGE

This simple table will help you understand the huge tax savings that Cyprus can offer you compared to corporate and personal taxation in major EU countries. It refers to profits equal to € 100,000 accrued by LTD incorporated in Cyprus with foreign income (e.g., online business) and distributed to non-dom individuals.

Description	Amount (€)	Percentage (%)
Corporate Profit	100,000	100%
Corporate Tax	12,500	12.5%
Profit after Corporate Tax	87,500	87.5%
Dividends Distributed	87,500	87.5%
Dividend Taxation for Non-Dom	0	0%
GHS Taxation on Dividends (2.65%)	2,318.75	2.65%
Total Taxes Paid	14,818.75	14.82%
Net Amount for Non-Dom Beneficiary	85,181.25	85.18%

In the following two chapters, we will delve into the corporate and personal aspects of taxation.

CHAPTER 3
TAXATION OF INDIVIDUALS UNDER THE NON-DOM REGIME

PERSONAL INCOME TAX

Cyprus employs a progressive income tax system for individuals, with tax rates that range from 0% to 35%. For residents, the first €19,500 of annual income is exempt from tax. This threshold provides a substantial benefit, particularly for those with lower incomes or those just entering the Cypriot job market. Beyond this threshold, the tax rates increase progressively:

- 20% for income between €19,501 and €28,000
- 25% for income between €28,001 and €36,300
- 30% for income between €36,301 and €60,000
- 35% for income above €60,000

For individuals with non-dom status, the tax advantages become even more pronounced. **Non-doms are primarily concerned with treating foreign-sourced income, which, under the non-dom regime, can be exempt from Cyprus taxation.** This regime allows non-doms to earn significant income from foreign sources without incurring Cypriot tax liabilities, provided that the income is not remitted to Cyprus.

In addition to the exemptions on foreign income, Cyprus offers various allowances and deductions that further reduce taxable income. These include contributions to social insurance, pension funds, and other approved funds. Similarly, payments to approved medical funds and contributions to trade unions or professional bodies are also deductible.

Moreover, non-doms can benefit from specific tax incentives designed to attract foreign talent and investment. For instance, expatriates moving to Cyprus for employment can benefit from a 50% tax exemption on their employment income if their annual salary exceeds €100,000. This exemption applies for a period of ten years, provided that the individual was not a tax resident in Cyprus for the five tax years preceding the commencement of employment and was not a tax resident in Cyprus in the year preceding the commencement of employment.

Non-doms can also use the Notional Interest Deduction (NID) on new equity introduced into a company. The non-dom regime in Cyprus also provides tax benefits related to pension income.

DIVIDEND AND INTEREST INCOME

One of the most significant advantages of the non-dom regime is the exemption from the Special Defence Contribution (SDC) on foreign-sourced dividends and interest income. For dividend income, this exemption means that non-doms can receive dividends from their international investments without incurring additional Cypriot taxes.

Similarly, interest income earned from foreign sources is also exempt from SDC for non-doms. This exemption covers interest from various sources, including bank deposits, bonds, and other interest-bearing instruments held outside Cyprus.

In addition to the exemptions on foreign-sourced dividends and interest income, Cyprus also offers favorable tax treatment for local dividends and interest income. Dividends received from Cypriot companies are generally exempt from income tax but are subject to

SDC at a rate of 17%. However, under the non-dom regime, non-doms are exempt from SDC on both local and foreign dividends, provided the dividends are not received from companies engaged in activities listed as non-exempt under the SDC law.

Interest income from local sources is typically subject to SDC at a rate of 30%. However, non-doms are also exempt from SDC on local interest income.

Moreover, the non-dom regime provides investors with a stable and predictable tax environment. The Cypriot government has shown a solid commitment to maintaining and enhancing the attractiveness of the non-dom regime, ensuring that the tax benefits remain consistent and reliable.

CAPITAL GAINS AND OTHER TAXABLE INCOME

One of Cyprus's most significant benefits of the non-dom regime is the favorable tax treatment of capital gains. In Cyprus, capital gains tax is generally imposed only on gains arising from the disposal of immovable property located in Cyprus or on the disposal of shares in companies that own such immovable property. This means that capital gains from the sale of foreign securities, such as shares and bonds, are not subject to capital gains tax in Cyprus.

In addition to exempting capital gains from foreign securities, Cyprus offers favorable tax treatment for other forms of taxable income. For example, rental income from properties located outside Cyprus is exempt from the Special Defence Contribution (SDC) for non-doms. Non-doms are subject to SDC for rental income earned from properties located in Cyprus. However, they can still benefit from various allowances and deductions that reduce their overall tax liability. These include deductions for expenses related to the maintenance and repair of the property, as well as mortgage interest deductions.

Other types of taxable income, such as royalties and intellectual property income, also receive favorable tax treatment under the non-dom regime. Furthermore, Cyprus provides various tax incentives and allowances that benefit non-doms with other taxable income: deductions for charitable donations, contributions to approved pension and medical funds, and allowances for dependent children and spouses.

CHAPTER 4
CORPORATE TAXATION IN CYPRUS

OVERVIEW OF CORPORATE TAX RATES AND REGULATIONS

The cornerstone of the Cypriot corporate tax system is its corporate tax rate, which, at 12.5%, is one of the lowest in the European Union. This competitive rate applies uniformly to both domestic and international companies, making Cyprus an attractive location for businesses looking to minimize their tax liabilities.

The Cypriot corporate tax framework is based on a Worldwide system, which means that if a company is considered resident in Cyprus, it is taxed on its worldwide income, regardless of where it is generated. Nonresident companies, on the other hand, are taxed only on Cyprus-source income.

In addition to the low corporate tax rate, Cyprus offers various exemptions, deductions, and allowances that further reduce the effective tax burden on businesses. These include exemptions on dividend income, profits from overseas permanent establishments, and certain types of interest income. The Cypriot tax system also allows for the deduction of business expenses, including interest on loans, depreciation of assets, and costs associated with research and development.

Dividend income received by a Cyprus-resident company from another Cyprus-resident company is exempt from corporate tax, promoting reinvestment within the local economy. Additionally, dividends received from foreign subsidiaries are exempt from corporate tax, provided the paying company engages in more than 50% of activities generating passive income or the foreign tax burden is not significantly lower than that of Cyprus. This exemption aligns Cyprus's tax system with international standards and ensures that businesses are not subjected to double taxation on their dividend income.

Interest income is generally subject to corporate tax; however, notable exceptions exist. For example, interest income earned in the ordinary course of business, such as by banks and financial institutions, is taxed as business income. Conversely, interest income not arising from ordinary business activities, such as interest on bank deposits and loans to third parties, is subject to Special Defence Contribution (SDC) at a rate of 30%. This dual approach to interest income taxation ensures that different types of income are taxed appropriately, aligning with the nature of the business activities.

The taxation of capital gains in Cyprus is another area where the tax system provides significant advantages. Generally, capital gains are exempt from corporate tax unless they arise from the disposal of immovable property located in Cyprus or shares in companies holding such property.

Cyprus has also implemented an Intellectual Property (IP) Box regime, which offers substantial tax benefits for income derived from qualifying IP assets. Under this regime, 80% of the qualifying profits from IP assets are exempt from taxation, resulting in an effective tax rate of just 2.5%. This regime encourages innovation and intellectual property development in Cyprus, making it an attractive jurisdiction for research and development activities.

The regulatory framework governing corporate taxation in Cyprus is designed to be transparent and straightforward, ensuring businesses can easily navigate the tax system. The Cyprus Tax Department provides comprehensive guidance and support to businesses, helping them understand their tax obligations and comply with the relevant regulations. The tax authorities in Cyprus are known for their professionalism and responsiveness, ensuring that businesses can resolve any tax issues promptly and efficiently.

Cyprus's commitment to international tax transparency and cooperation further enhances the credibility and attractiveness of its corporate tax system. Cyprus is a signatory to various international agreements, including the OECD's Common Reporting Standard (CRS) and the Base Erosion and Profit Shifting (BEPS) initiative. These agreements require Cyprus to exchange financial information with other jurisdictions and implement measures to combat tax evasion and aggressive tax planning. By adhering to these international standards, Cyprus ensures that its tax system remains robust, transparent, and compliant with global norms.

TAX RESIDENCY FOR COMPANIES

Tax residency is critical in determining a company's tax obligations in Cyprus. Under Cypriot law, a company is considered a tax resident if its management and control are exercised in Cyprus. This concept of management and control is broadly interpreted. Generally, it includes the place where the board of directors meets and makes decisions and where the company's key management and commercial decisions necessary for the conduct of its business as a whole are made.

The determination of tax residency based on management and control provides a flexible and practical framework that aligns with international tax principles. This approach allows companies to establish tax residency in Cyprus without requiring extensive physical presence or operational activities within the country, making it particularly attractive for holding companies and international business structures.

Once a company is established as a tax resident in Cyprus, it is subject to Cypriot corporate tax on its worldwide income.

In practice, the process of establishing tax residency involves several steps. Initially, the company must be incorporated in Cyprus, which involves registering with the Registrar of Companies and obtaining a certificate of incorporation. This process is relatively straightforward and can be completed within a few days, thanks to the efficient and business-friendly regulatory environment in Cyprus.

Following incorporation, the company must demonstrate that its management and control are exercised in Cyprus. This typically involves holding regular board meetings in Cyprus, appointing local directors, and ensuring that key management decisions are made within the country. Maintaining proper documentation, such as minutes of board meetings and records of decisions, is essential to substantiate the company's tax residency status.

Additionally, the company may need to establish a physical presence in Cyprus, such as an office or registered address, to support its claim of management and control. While the physical presence requirement is generally minimal, it helps reinforce the company's connection to Cyprus and provides a basis for claiming tax residency.

Choosing to establish a physical presence in Cyprus, even if only with an office or home office, makes it possible to obtain valuable documents to show as proof of residency to banking institutions and marketplaces, increasingly due in part to stringent European regulations (see DAC7), due-diligence on operators of online businesses requires the periodic submission of bills and invoices attesting to one's physical residence and that of the company at the addresses indicated in the company documents at the registered office or operational headquarters of the company.

Once tax residency is established, the company must register with the Cyprus Tax Department and obtain a tax identification number. This straightforward registration process involves submitting the necessary forms and documentation to the tax authorities. The company will then be subject to Cypriot corporate tax on its worldwide income, benefiting from the various exemptions, deductions, and allowances available under Cypriot tax law.

Maintaining tax residency in Cyprus requires ongoing compliance with local regulations and tax obligations. This includes filing annual tax returns, paying corporate taxes, and adhering to other reporting requirements. The Cypriot tax authorities provide comprehensive guidance and support to help companies meet their compliance obligations and ensure that they can operate efficiently within the tax framework.

The concept of tax residency based on management and control also aligns with international best practices and helps prevent issues related to tax avoidance and base erosion. By requiring companies to demonstrate substantive management and control activities in Cyprus, the tax residency rules ensure that only genuinely established businesses can benefit from the favorable tax regime. This approach enhances the credibility and integrity of the Cypriot tax system, making it a reliable and attractive jurisdiction for international business operations.

TAX BENEFITS FOR CORPORATIONS

One of the most significant tax benefits for corporations in Cyprus is the exemption on dividend income. As mentioned earlier, dividends received by a Cyprus-resident company from another Cyprus-resident company are exempt from corporate tax. Additionally, dividends received from foreign subsidiaries are exempt from corporate tax, provided certain conditions are met. This exemption helps prevent double taxation of dividend income and encourages the repatriation of profits to Cyprus.

The Notional Interest Deduction (NID) is another valuable tax benefit available to corporations in Cyprus. The NID allows companies to deduct a notional interest expense on new equity introduced into the business from their taxable income. The notional interest is calculated based on the reference interest rate set by the Central Bank of Cyprus, plus a premium. This deduction helps reduce the effective tax rate on corporate profits and encourages businesses to invest in equity financing rather than relying solely on debt.

Cyprus also offers tax incentives for research and development (R&D) activities. Companies engaged in R&D can benefit from enhanced tax deductions for qualifying expenses, including salaries of researchers, costs of materials and supplies, and expenses related to developing new products and technologies. These incentives are designed to promote innovation and support the growth of high-tech industries in Cyprus, making it an attractive location for businesses involved in R&D activities.

The Intellectual Property (IP) Box regime is another key tax benefit for businesses in Cyprus. Under this regime, qualified profits from intellectual property assets, such as patents and copyrighted software (even developed in-house), are subject to an effective tax rate of just 2.5 percent.

Cyprus also offers opportunities for deductions for business expenses, such as depreciation of assets, interest on loans, and costs related to marketing and promotion. Businesses can also benefit from tax incentives for investments in specific sectors, such as renewable energy, tourism, and shipping.

CHAPTER 5
RELOCATING A COMPANY TO CYPRUS

LEGAL AND ADMINISTRATIVE STEPS

One of the first steps in relocating a company to Cyprus is understanding the legal implications of re-domiciliation. Cyprus law allows foreign companies to transfer their registered office to Cyprus without dissolving the original company or incorporating a new entity. This process, known as re-domiciliation, is governed by the Companies Law Cap. 113, specifically under Sections 354A to 354P. The law permits companies registered in jurisdictions that allow re-domiciliation to apply for registration as a continuing entity in Cyprus.

The re-domiciliation process begins with submitting a formal application to the Registrar of Companies in Cyprus. The application must include several key documents, including a resolution from the company's board of directors approving the relocation, a declaration of solvency, and evidence that the company is in good standing in its original jurisdiction. Additionally, the company must provide its current memorandum, articles of association, and any necessary amendments to comply with Cyprus law.

One crucial aspect of the re-domiciliation process is ensuring that the company's name is not already used in Cyprus. If the name is available, the company can retain its original name; otherwise, it may need to choose a new name that complies with the naming conventions in Cyprus.

Once the application and accompanying documents are submitted and reviewed, the Registrar of Companies will issue a temporary certificate of continuation, which allows the company to operate in Cyprus. At the same time, the final steps of re-domiciliation are completed.

Upon receiving the temporary certificate, the company must publish a notice of its relocation in two daily newspapers in Cyprus within 14 days. This publication serves as a public announcement of the company's intention to relocate and allows any objections to be raised. Suppose no objections are received, and the company has complied with all necessary legal requirements. In that case, the Registrar will issue a final certificate of continuation, officially recognizing the company as a Cyprus-registered entity.

The final certificate of continuation marks the completion of the re-domiciliation process, and the company is now subject to Cyprus's legal and tax framework. This includes compliance with local corporate governance requirements, such as maintaining a registered office in Cyprus, appointing local directors, and keeping statutory books and records within the country. Additionally, the company must adhere to Cyprus's annual reporting obligations, including the submission of financial statements, tax returns, and other regulatory filings.

INCORPORATE A NEW COMPANY

In addition to re-domiciliation, another option for transferring a company to Cyprus is incorporating a new legal entity. The incorporation process is relatively simple and involves submitting the necessary incorporation documents to the Registrar of Companies (articles of incorporation, articles of association of the company, declaration of compliance, details of directors, shareholders, and from the registered office). The incorporation process usually takes a few days, after which the company will receive a certificate of incorporation.

The first step in setting up a business in Cyprus is selecting the appropriate legal structure. The most common types of business entities in

Cyprus include limited liability companies (LLCs), public limited companies (PLCs), partnerships, and sole proprietorships. The choice of business structure depends on several factors, including the size of the business, the number of shareholders, and the nature of the business activities.

Limited liability companies (LLCs) are Cyprus's most popular business structure, particularly for small and medium-sized enterprises (SMEs). An LLC can be established with a minimum of one shareholder and one director, who can be the same person. The liability of shareholders is limited to their capital contributions, protecting against personal liability for the company's debts and obligations. LLCs are also subject to relatively simple corporate governance requirements, making them an attractive option for businesses seeking a straightforward and flexible structure.

On the other hand, public limited companies (PLCs) are more suitable for larger businesses that intend to raise capital from the public through the issuance of shares. A PLC must have at least seven shareholders and a minimum share capital of €25,630. PLCs are subject to more stringent regulatory requirements, including the obligation to hold annual general meetings, appoint a company secretary, and maintain a higher level of financial transparency. Despite these additional requirements, PLCs offer access to capital markets, which can significantly benefit businesses with ambitious growth plans.

In addition to choosing the legal structure, businesses must also register with the relevant authorities to obtain the necessary permits and licenses. The specific permits and licenses required depend on the nature of the business activities and the industry in which the company operates. For example, businesses engaged in financial services, telecommunications, or energy may require sector-specific licenses from regulatory bodies such as the Cyprus Securities and Exchange Commission (CySEC), the Cyprus Energy Regulatory Authority (CERA), or the Department of Electronic Communications.

One of the key steps in setting up a business in Cyprus is opening a corporate bank account. Cyprus has a well-developed banking sector with several local and international banks offering various financial services. To open a corporate bank account, the company must provide multiple documents, including the certificate of incorporation, the memorandum and articles of association, the resolution of the board of directors authorizing the account opening, and identification documents for the directors and shareholders. Additionally, banks may require proof of the company's business activities and the source of funds as part of their due diligence procedures.

Once the corporate bank account is established, the company can conduct business transactions in Cyprus. It is essential to maintain proper accounting records and financial statements in accordance with Cyprus's financial reporting standards, which are based on International Financial Reporting Standards (IFRS). Companies must also register for Value Added Tax (VAT) if their annual turnover exceeds the VAT registration threshold, currently set at €15,600. VAT registration is a crucial step for businesses involved in the sale of goods and services, as it allows them to charge VAT on their sales and reclaim VAT on their purchases.

In addition to VAT registration, businesses in Cyprus may also be required to register with the Social Insurance Department to comply with employment regulations. Employers are required to make social insurance contributions on behalf of their employees, covering benefits such as pensions, unemployment insurance, and healthcare. The contributions are calculated as a percentage of the employee's gross salary and are shared between the employer, the employee, and the government.

TRUST COMPANIES AS SHAREHOLDERS AND DIRECTORS

In Cyprus, it is permissible to appoint a trust company to hold shares on behalf of the beneficial owners (the true owners of the company) and to act as a company director. This structure can provide significant privacy benefits, as the trust company's details will appear on the public register of the Cyprus Registrar of Companies rather than the names of the individual beneficial owners.

Privacy and Confidentiality

One of the primary reasons for using a trust company as both shareholder and director is to protect the privacy of the beneficial owners. In Cyprus, while specific company details are publicly accessible, the use of a trust company means that the names of the beneficial owners are not disclosed in the public register.

The trust company holds the shares under a trust arrangement, where the beneficial owner is the true owner, but the trust company acts on their behalf. Similarly, when a Trust Company is appointed as a director, it acts in the capacity of a nominee, managing the company's affairs according to the instructions of the beneficial owners while maintaining their anonymity.

Meeting Residency Requirements

For a company to be considered a tax resident in Cyprus, it must be "managed and controlled" from within Cyprus. This generally means that most of the company's directors should reside in Cyprus, and board meetings should ideally be held in Cyprus. Using a trust company to fulfill the director role is particularly useful if the beneficial owners are not yet resident or domiciled in Cyprus.

Facilitating Company Incorporation Before Relocation

Utilizing a trust company as a director and shareholder is advantageous for individuals or businesses looking to establish a company in Cyprus before relocating. As the company must have its management and control in Cyprus to be deemed a tax resident, the trust company can promptly meet this criteria, allowing the company to commence operations without delay. This arrangement is particularly useful for businesses that want to establish a legal entity in Cyprus to secure contracts, set up operations, or start trading before the beneficial owners move to Cyprus.

Ensuring Compliance and Proper Corporate Governance

Appointing a trust company as a director also ensures that the company adheres to local legal and regulatory requirements. Trust companies in Cyprus are typically well-versed in local corporate governance standards, compliance obligations, and tax regulations.

Flexibility in Business Management

Using a trust company as a director offers flexibility in managing the company. The trust company can act based on the specific instructions of the beneficial owners, who may be located abroad. This allows the beneficial owners to maintain effective control over the company's decisions and operations, even if they are not physically present in Cyprus.

When beneficial owners decide to relocate to Cyprus, they can take over the directorship roles personally if they wish to have more direct involvement in the company's management. Alternatively, they can continue to use the trust company for ongoing privacy and convenience.

How It Works in Practice

When setting up a company in Cyprus using a trust company, the process generally involves the following steps:

1. **Selection of the Trust Company**: The beneficial owners select a reputable trust company in Cyprus that will act as the shareholder and/or director.
2. **Incorporation of the Company**: The trust company incorporates the new company with the Registrar of Companies. The trust company's name appears as the shareholder and/or director in the incorporation documents.
3. **Trust Deed and Nominee Agreement**: A trust deed or nominee agreement is executed between the trust company and the beneficial owners. This document outlines the trust company's obligations, including acting on behalf of the beneficial owners according to their instructions.
4. **Corporate Bank Account Opening**: Once the company is incorporated, the trust company can assist in opening a corporate bank account in Cyprus. The trust company can operate the bank account on behalf of the beneficial owners, or the beneficial owners can be granted direct access.
5. **Ongoing Management and Compliance**: The trust company handles the day-to-day management and ensures compliance

with all legal, tax, and corporate governance requirements. The beneficial owners receive regular updates and can provide instructions as needed.
6. **Relocation and Transition**: If the beneficial owners eventually relocate to Cyprus, they can gradually transition into more active roles within the company, if desired, or continue to rely on the trust company for ongoing management.

HIRING EMPLOYEES

Cyprus boasts a highly educated and multilingual workforce with a high proficiency in English, which is widely used in business and legal transactions. The country's robust education system and the presence of several universities and technical institutes ensure a steady supply of qualified professionals in various fields, including finance, law, engineering, and information technology.

When hiring employees in Cyprus, businesses must comply with local labor laws regulating employment contracts, working hours, minimum wages, and employee benefits. Employment contracts must be in writing and specify the terms and conditions of employment, including the job title, salary, working hours, and leave entitlements. Employers must also provide employees with a written statement of their rights and obligations under Cyprus labor law.

Cyprus labor law provides strong protection for employees, particularly regarding job security and workplace conditions. For example, employees are entitled to a minimum of 20 days of paid annual leave per year, in addition to public holidays. The law also limits working hours, with a standard working week of 40 hours and overtime compensated at higher rates. Employers must also provide a safe and healthy work environment that complies with occupational health and safety regulations.

In terms of employee benefits, Cyprus offers a comprehensive social security system that provides various benefits, including old-age pensions, disability benefits, maternity benefits, and unemployment insurance. Employers are required to make contributions to the social insurance fund on behalf of their employees, and employees are also required to contribute a percentage of their salary to the fund. The social insurance system is administered by the Social Insurance Department, which oversees the collection of contributions and the payment of benefits.

In addition to the statutory benefits, many employers in Cyprus offer additional benefits to attract and retain talent, such as private health insurance, pension schemes, and performance-based bonuses. These benefits can be crucial in attracting skilled professionals, particularly in competitive industries such as finance and technology.

CHAPTER 6
VAT AND OTHER INDIRECT TAXES IN CYPRUS

OVERVIEW OF VAT SYSTEM

Value Added Tax (VAT) is a crucial component of the tax system in Cyprus, representing a significant source of revenue for the government. The VAT system in Cyprus is aligned with the European Union VAT directives, ensuring consistency and compliance with EU standards. The VAT in Cyprus is designed to be straightforward and transparent, making it easier for businesses to comply with their tax obligations.

The standard VAT rate in Cyprus is set at 19%, which is relatively moderate compared to other EU countries. This rate applies to most goods and services supplied within Cyprus. However, Cyprus also implements reduced VAT rates for specific categories of goods and services to alleviate the tax burden on essential and socially important items. The reduced rates are as follows:

- A reduced rate of 9% applies to services such as restaurant and catering services, hotel accommodation, and transport of passengers and their accompanying luggage within Cyprus.
- A reduced rate of 5% applies to essential goods such as foodstuffs, pharmaceuticals, books, newspapers, certain

cultural and sporting events, and specific services for disabled persons.

Additionally, certain goods and services are exempt from VAT altogether. These exemptions include financial services, medical and dental care, education, insurance services, and leasing immovable property (with some exceptions). The VAT exemptions are intended to reduce the cost of these essential services for consumers and ensure they remain affordable.

The VAT system in Cyprus also includes provisions for 0% rate supplies. This category primarily includes exports of goods and related services, international transport services, and intra-community supplies of goods to other EU member states.

VAT REGISTRATION AND COMPLIANCE

VAT registration is mandatory for businesses operating in Cyprus that exceed certain turnover thresholds. The standard threshold for mandatory VAT registration is €15,600 per year. Businesses exceeding this threshold must register for VAT with the Cyprus Tax Department and charge VAT on their taxable supplies. However, businesses with a turnover below this threshold can also choose to register voluntarily, allowing them to reclaim input VAT on their purchases and expenses.

The VAT registration process involves applying to the Cyprus Tax Department providing details about the business, its activities, and its estimated turnover. The application must be accompanied by supporting documentation, such as a certificate of incorporation, business licenses, and identification documents of the company's directors and shareholders. Once the application is approved, the business is issued a VAT registration number, which must be displayed on all invoices and tax documents.

Once registered for VAT, businesses must comply with various reporting and compliance requirements. These include submitting periodic VAT returns, usually quarterly, detailing the VAT collected on sales (output VAT) and the VAT paid on purchases (input VAT). The

VAT return must be submitted electronically through the Tax Department's online portal, along with any payment due. The deadline for submitting VAT returns and making payments is typically the 10th day of the second month following the end of the reporting period.

Businesses must also maintain accurate and comprehensive records of all transactions subject to VAT. This includes keeping copies of invoices issued and received, receipts, and other relevant documents. These records must be retained for at least six years and be made available for inspection by the Tax Department if required. Proper record-keeping is essential for ensuring compliance with VAT laws and facilitating audits and reviews by the tax authorities.

In addition to standard VAT returns, businesses engaged in cross-border trade within the EU are required to submit supplementary declarations, such as the EC Sales List (ECSL) and the Intrastat declarations. The ECSL provides details of intra-community goods and services supplies to VAT-registered customers in other EU member states. The Intrastat declaration collects statistical data on the movement of goods between EU member states, helping to monitor and analyze intra-EU trade.

OTHER INDIRECT TAXES AND DUTIES

In addition to VAT, Cyprus imposes various other indirect taxes and duties that businesses and individuals must be aware of.

Excise duties are taxes levied on specific goods, such as alcohol, tobacco, and energy products. These duties are designed to raise revenue and discourage the consumption of certain goods that are deemed harmful to health or the environment. The rates of excise duties vary depending on the product type and its classification under the relevant legislation.

For example, excise duties on alcohol are calculated based on the type and strength of the alcoholic beverage. Spirits and distilled beverages typically attract higher duty rates than beer and wine. Tobacco products, including cigarettes, cigars, and loose tobacco, are also subject to excise duties, which are calculated based on the quantity and type of product. Energy products, such as gasoline, diesel, and heating fuel, are subject to excise duties to promote energy efficiency and reduce environmental impact.

Import duties are taxes levied on goods imported into Cyprus from non-EU countries. These duties are designed to protect local industries and raise revenue from international trade. The rates of import duties vary depending on the type of product and its classification under the Harmonized System (HS) code. In addition to import duties, imported goods may be subject to VAT and excise duties, depending on their nature.

To facilitate international trade, Cyprus has implemented various customs procedures and trade facilitation measures. These include the Authorized Economic Operator (AEO) program, which provides benefits such as simplified customs procedures and reduced inspection rates for compliant businesses. The Cyprus Customs and Excise Department is responsible for administering import duties and ensuring compliance with customs regulations.

Environmental taxes are designed to promote sustainable development and protect the environment by taxing activities that have a negative impact on the environment. In Cyprus, environmental taxes are levied on products and activities such as plastic bags, waste disposal, and vehicle emissions.

Other indirect taxes in Cyprus include stamp duty and transfer fees. Stamp duty is a tax levied on certain legal documents and transactions, such as contracts, leases, and transfer deeds. The stamp duty rates vary depending on the type and value of the transaction. Transfer fees are payable on the transfer of immovable property and are calculated based on the transferred property's value. These fees are designed to raise revenue from property transactions and contribute to the country's overall tax revenue.

CHAPTER 7
COMPLIANCE AND REPORTING REQUIREMENTS

ANNUAL TAX FILING OBLIGATIONS

For individuals, the tax year in Cyprus aligns with the calendar year, running from January 1 to December 31. Personal income tax returns must be filed by July 31 of the year following the tax year. However, if an individual is required to submit audited financial statements, the deadline extends to December 31. All residents with an annual income exceeding €19,500 must file a tax return, regardless of the source of income. This includes income from employment, self-employment, pensions, rental income, and investment income.

Self-employed individuals must submit a self-assessment tax return, which includes detailed information about their business income and expenses. They must also make provisional tax payments twice a year based on their annual taxable income estimate. The first installment is due by July 31, and the second by December 31. Any tax balance due is payable by August 1 of the following year after the final tax return is submitted.

For corporations, the tax year also runs from January 1 to December 31. Corporate tax returns must be filed by March 31 of the second year following the end of the tax year, allowing ample time for companies to prepare their financial statements and ensure accuracy. Corporations must also make provisional tax payments based on their estimated annual profits, with installments due on July 31, September 30, and December 31. Any final balance of tax due must be paid by August 1 of the following year.

In addition to the annual tax return, companies must submit audited financial statements prepared in accordance with International Financial Reporting Standards (IFRS). These statements must be audited by a licensed auditor in Cyprus, who will provide an independent opinion on the accuracy and completeness of the financial information presented. The audited financial statements, along with the tax return, form the basis for calculating the final corporate tax liability.

The annual tax filing obligations for businesses also include submitting specific forms and declarations related to VAT, payroll taxes, and other indirect taxes. For VAT, businesses must file periodic returns, usually on a quarterly basis, detailing the VAT collected on sales and the VAT paid on purchases. The VAT return must be submitted electronically through the Tax Department's online portal, along with any payment due.

Payroll tax obligations include the submission of monthly Pay-As-You-Earn (PAYE) returns detailing the income tax withheld from employees' salaries. Employers must also file an annual employer's return by July 31, summarizing the total salaries paid and the tax withheld during the year. This return must be accompanied by individual employee tax certificates, which employees use to file their personal tax returns.

Additional reporting requirements apply to businesses engaged in cross-border transactions. These include the submission of the EC Sales List (ECSL) and Intrastat declarations. The ECSL provides details of intra-community goods and services supplies to VAT-registered customers in other EU member states. At the same time, the Intrastat declaration collects statistical data on the movement of goods between EU member states.

AUDIT AND INSPECTION PROCESSES

The Cyprus Tax Department conducts audits and inspections to ensure compliance with tax laws and verify the accuracy of tax returns submitted by individuals and businesses. The audit and inspection processes are designed to detect and prevent tax evasion, ensure accurate reporting of income, and maintain the integrity of the tax system.

Audits can be conducted randomly or triggered by specific risk factors, such as discrepancies in tax returns, significant changes in income, or irregularities detected through data analysis. The audit process typically begins with a notification from the Tax Department, informing the taxpayer of the audit and requesting specific documentation and information.

The scope of an audit can vary depending on the complexity of the taxpayer's financial affairs and the issues identified by the Tax Department. For individuals, an audit may focus on verifying income from employment, self-employment, rental properties, and investments. This includes reviewing bank statements, invoices, receipts, and other supporting documents to ensure that all income has been accurately reported.

Audits are generally more comprehensive for businesses and may involve a detailed examination of financial statements, accounting records, and business transactions. The auditor will assess the accuracy of the reported income, expenses, and deductions and verify compliance with VAT, payroll tax, and other indirect tax obligations. This may include reconciling sales and purchase records, reviewing payroll records, and confirming the correct application of VAT rates.

During the audit, the taxpayer has the opportunity to provide explanations and additional documentation to support their tax return. Cooperation and transparency with the auditors can facilitate a smoother audit process and help resolve any issues more efficiently. Once the audit is completed, the Tax Department will issue an audit report detailing the findings and any adjustments to the taxpayer's tax liability.

In cases where significant discrepancies or evidence of tax evasion are found, the Tax Department may conduct more intensive investigations. This can involve interviews with the taxpayer and third parties, forensic analysis of financial records, and other investigative techniques. The goal is to uncover any hidden income, fraudulent activities, or other violations of tax laws.

Apart from audits initiated by the Tax Department, there are also special audits conducted under the directive of the European Union or international agreements. These audits aim to ensure compliance with international tax standards, such as the Common Reporting Standard (CRS) and the Base Erosion and Profit Shifting (BEPS) framework. Such audits often focus on cross-border transactions, transfer pricing, and the implementation of anti-avoidance measures.

Businesses must also be prepared for VAT inspections, which are conducted to verify compliance with VAT laws and regulations. VAT inspections typically involve reviewing sales and purchase records, VAT invoices, and VAT returns. The inspectors may visit the business premises to examine the physical inventory, verify the accuracy of stock records, and ensure that VAT is correctly applied and accounted for.

Compliance with audit and inspection processes requires maintaining accurate and comprehensive records of all financial transactions. Proper record-keeping is essential for substantiating income, expenses, and deductions and for demonstrating compliance with tax laws. As Cypriot law requires, businesses and individuals must retain these records for at least six years.

PENALTIES AND SANCTIONS FOR NON-COMPLIANCE

One of the most common penalties for non-compliance is the imposition of fines for late filing of tax returns. If an individual or business fails to submit their tax return by the required deadline, they may be subject to a fixed penalty. For personal income tax returns, the penalty for late filing is typically €100 if the return is submitted within six months of the deadline and €200 if submitted later than six months.

For corporate tax returns, the penalty is generally €100 for late submission within six months and €200 after that.

In addition to fines for late filing, there are also penalties for late payment of taxes. If taxpayers fail to pay their tax liability by the due date, they may be subject to interest charges on the outstanding amount. The Ministry of Finance sets the interest rate at 3.5% per annum. Interest is calculated daily from the due date until the tax is paid in full.

More severe penalties apply in cases of tax evasion or fraudulent activities. Tax evasion involves deliberately underreporting income, inflating deductions, or engaging in other deceptive practices to reduce tax liability. If the Tax Department detects tax evasion during an audit or investigation, the taxpayer may be subject to significant financial penalties, calculated as a percentage of the underpaid tax. These penalties can range from 10% to 50% of the tax due, depending on the severity of the violation.

In serious tax evasion or fraud cases, criminal charges may be brought against the taxpayer. This can result in prosecution, and if convicted, the taxpayer may face imprisonment, substantial fines, or both. The Tax Department works closely with law enforcement agencies to investigate and prosecute serious tax offenses, ensuring that offenders are held accountable and that the integrity of the tax system is upheld.

Businesses that fail to comply with VAT obligations may also face specific penalties. For example, failure to register for VAT when required can result in a fine of up to €85 for each month of non-registration. Failure to submit VAT returns or pay VAT due can attract penalties and interest charges similar to those for income tax. Businesses that issue incorrect or fraudulent VAT invoices may also be subject to further fines and sanctions.

In addition to financial penalties, the Tax Department may impose other administrative measures to enforce compliance. This can include garnishing wages or bank accounts, placing liens on property, and seizing assets to recover unpaid taxes. These measures are typically used as a last resort when other attempts to collect the tax have failed.

Businesses and individuals must fully comply with their tax obligations to avoid penalties and sanctions. This involves timely filing of tax returns, accurate reporting of income and expenses, and prompt payment of taxes due. Proper record-keeping is essential for substantiating tax returns and demonstrating compliance during audits and inspections.

CHAPTER 8
TAX PLANNING AND CASE STUDIES

ROLE OF TAX ADVISORS IN CYPRUS

One of the primary responsibilities of tax advisors is to guide tax compliance. This involves helping clients understand their tax obligations, including filing requirements, payment deadlines, and the documentation needed to substantiate their tax returns. Advisors ensure that all necessary forms and returns are accurately completed and submitted on time, minimizing the risk of penalties and interest charges for late filing or payment. For businesses, this includes assistance with corporate tax returns, VAT returns, payroll tax filings, and other statutory declarations. In addition to tax planning and compliance, tax advisors provide representation and support during audits and inspections conducted by the Cyprus Tax Department. This involves preparing clients for audits, gathering and organizing the required documentation, and liaising with tax authorities on behalf of the client. Advisors can help clarify complex tax issues, resolve discrepancies, and negotiate settlements, ensuring that the audit process is as smooth and efficient as possible.

DEVELOPING A TAX-EFFICIENT CORPORATE STRUCTURE

Examining case studies and best practices can provide valuable insights into the effective implementation of tax planning strategies and the development of tax-efficient corporate structures. This section presents several case studies of businesses that have successfully leveraged Cyprus's favorable tax regime, along with best practices for achieving optimal tax outcomes.

Case Study 1: Multinational Holding Company

A multinational corporation with subsidiaries in various countries established a holding company in Cyprus to manage its global investments. The primary objective was to optimize the repatriation of profits and reduce dividend withholding taxes.

Strategy:

- The holding company was structured to take advantage of Cyprus's exemption on dividend income received from foreign subsidiaries.
- The company benefited from the extensive network of double taxation treaties by centralizing the ownership of international subsidiaries in Cyprus, reducing withholding taxes on cross-border dividend payments.
- The holding company also utilized the Notional Interest Deduction (NID) on new equity to reduce its taxable income, further enhancing tax efficiency.

Outcome:

- The company achieved significant tax savings on dividends received from foreign subsidiaries.
- The centralized structure streamlined the management of global investments and improved overall financial efficiency.
- Using the NID reduced the effective tax rate, lowering overall tax liabilities.

Case Study 2: Intellectual Property (IP) Holding Company

A technology company specializing in software development and innovation established an IP holding company in Cyprus to manage its intellectual property assets.

Strategy:

- The IP holding company was structured to benefit from the IP Box regime, which offers a reduced tax rate of 2.5% on qualifying IP income.
- The company centralized the ownership and management of its IP assets in Cyprus, including patents and software copyrights.
- Royalties and licensing fees generated from the commercialization of the IP assets were channeled through the IP holding company.

Outcome:

- The company achieved substantial tax savings on IP income, enhancing the profitability of its innovation activities.
- The centralized IP management structure facilitated the efficient commercialization of IP assets globally.
- The favorable tax treatment supported the company's strategic goals and long-term growth objectives.

Case Study 3: Intra-Group Financing and Treasury Center

A large multinational corporation operating in multiple countries established a financing and treasury center in Cyprus to manage its funding intra-group and treasury activities.

Strategy:

- The financing and treasury center was structured to take advantage of Cyprus's favorable tax treatment of interest income.

- The company utilized the Notional Interest Deduction (NID) on new equity introduced into the financing center to reduce its taxable income.
- The center managed the group's financing activities, including intra-group loans, cash pooling, and foreign exchange risk management.

Outcome:

- The financing and treasury center achieved significant tax savings on interest income, reducing the overall cost of capital for the corporate group.
- Centralizing financing and treasury activities improved financial efficiency and optimized cash flow.
- The strategic use of the NID enhanced the tax efficiency of the financing structure, supporting the company's global financial strategy.

Case Study 4: E-commerce Company Utilizing Amazon FBA

A Cyprus-based e-commerce company that sells products on Amazon using the Fulfillment by Amazon (FBA) service leveraged Cyprus's non-dom regime and strategic VAT planning to optimize its tax liabilities while managing inventory across multiple EU countries.

Background:

The company sells various consumer products through Amazon's European marketplaces. To facilitate quick delivery to customers, the company uses Amazon's FBA service, which involves storing products in Amazon's fulfillment centers located in various EU countries. Consequently, the company has VAT registrations in several EU countries to comply with local tax regulations.

Strategy:

- The company established its headquarters in Cyprus to exploit the non-dom regime and favorable corporate tax environment.

- As a non-dom company, it focused on ensuring that foreign-sourced income (outside Cyprus) would be exempt from Cypriot taxation.
- The company registered for VAT in multiple EU countries where Amazon warehouses its inventory, ensuring compliance with local VAT regulations for sales and storage.
- It utilized the VAT One Stop Shop (OSS) scheme to simplify VAT compliance across the EU for digital services while managing physical goods through local VAT registrations.

Implementation:

The company set up its main corporate office in Cyprus, ensuring that key management and control activities were conducted within the country to maintain non-dom status. This included board meetings, strategic decision-making processes, and financial management activities.

VAT Registration and Compliance:

- The company registered for VAT in all EU countries where Amazon FBA warehouses were located. This ensured that it could manage VAT obligations related to stocking and shipping products from these locations.
- It utilized the VAT OSS (One Stop Shop) scheme for EU-wide sales to non-business customers, simplifying VAT reporting and payments for these transactions.
- Regular VAT returns were filed in each country, detailing the VAT collected on sales and paid on local expenses.

Inventory and Logistics Management:

- By leveraging Amazon FBA, the company optimized its inventory distribution to ensure fast delivery to customers across Europe. Based on sales data and demand forecasts, Inventory was placed in crucial Amazon fulfillment centers.

- The company maintained detailed inventory movements and transaction records to comply with VAT regulations and support tax audits if necessary.

Outcome:

- **Tax Efficiency:** The company achieved significant tax savings by taking advantage of Cyprus's non-dom regime, ensuring that its foreign-sourced income was exempt from Cypriot taxation. The effective corporate tax rate was minimized, enhancing overall profitability.
- **Simplified VAT Compliance:** Using the VAT OSS scheme and maintaining local VAT registrations, the company streamlined its VAT compliance processes, reducing administrative burdens and ensuring timely VAT payments.
- **Optimized Inventory Management:** Leveraging Amazon FBA allowed the company to offer fast delivery to customers across Europe, improving customer satisfaction and boosting sales.
- **Regulatory Compliance:** The company's proactive approach to VAT registration and transfer pricing compliance ensured that it remained in good standing with tax authorities across multiple jurisdictions, minimizing the risk of audits and penalties.

CHAPTER 9
EXPAT LIFE IN CYPRUS

MOVING TO CYPRUS

Relocating to Cyprus is a relatively straightforward process, thanks to the country's well-developed infrastructure and welcoming environment for expatriates. The first step for most expats is arriving in Cyprus via one of its two major international airports: Larnaca International Airport and Paphos International Airport. These airports are well-connected to numerous global destinations, making it easy for expats to travel to and from Cyprus.

Upon arrival, expats will typically arrange temporary accommodation while they search for a more permanent place to live. There are numerous options for temporary housing, including hotels, serviced apartments, and short-term rental properties. Many expats use the services of local real estate agents who can assist in finding suitable long-term housing based on their preferences and budgets.

Moving personal belongings to Cyprus is also manageable, with several international moving companies offering services to transport household goods and personal items. Cyprus's ports, particularly Limassol, are crucial shipment entry points. Expats should familiarize themselves with customs regulations, especially regarding the importation of vehicles, which may be subject to specific taxes and duties. It should be remembered that driving in Cyprus is left-hand drive, so motor vehicles used for right-hand drive may be impractical on the island.

MAIN ZONES TO LIVE IN CYPRUS

Cyprus, with its rich history, beautiful landscapes, and welcoming climate, offers a variety of living environments to suit different preferences and lifestyles. Cyprus offers something, whether seeking a bustling urban atmosphere, a tranquil beachside retreat, or a quiet rural setting.

The island is broadly divided into several vital zones, each with its own distinct characteristics:

Nicosia

Nicosia, the capital city of Cyprus, is the island's political and economic hub. It is the largest city and is known for its vibrant culture, historical significance, and modern amenities. Nicosia offers a cosmopolitan lifestyle with a mix of traditional and contemporary elements. The city is home to numerous international businesses, making it a popular choice for expatriates working in finance, law, and other professional sectors.

Aerial view of the historic center of Nicosia

Living in Nicosia provides access to top-tier educational institutions, healthcare facilities, shopping centers, and cultural attractions, including museums, theaters, and art galleries. The city's central location also makes traveling to other island parts convenient.

Limassol

Limassol, located on the southern coast of Cyprus, is the island's second-largest city and a significant business center. It is particularly popular among expatriates due to its thriving international community, modern infrastructure, and vibrant social scene. Limassol is known for its beautiful beachfront, luxury marinas, and extensive entertainment options, including fine dining, shopping, and nightlife.

Aerial view of the Limassol waterfront

The city is also a hub for the shipping industry and finance and technology sectors. Limassol offers a mix of residential options, from luxury apartments in the city center to quieter suburban neighborhoods, making it a versatile choice for different lifestyles.

Larnaca

Larnaca is a coastal city located on the southeast coast of Cyprus, known for its relaxed atmosphere, historical sites, and beautiful beaches. It is home to the island's main international airport, making it a convenient location for frequent travelers. Larnaca blends traditional Cypriot culture and modern amenities with various restaurants, cafes, and shops along its famous Finikoudes promenade.

Aerial view of Larnaca

The city is famous among expatriates who prefer a more laid-back lifestyle while still enjoying access to urban conveniences. Larnaca's residential areas range from beachfront apartments to suburban homes, catering to different housing preferences.

Paphos

Paphos, situated on the western coast of Cyprus, is a UNESCO World Heritage site known for its archaeological treasures, including ancient ruins and mosaics. The city has a growing expatriate community, particularly among those seeking a slower pace of life. Paphos offers a peaceful living environment with stunning coastal views, beautiful countryside, and a rich cultural heritage.

Aera view of the Paphos seaside promenade

The city has various residential options, from luxury villas to traditional Cypriot homes, often with breathtaking views of the Mediterranean Sea. Paphos also has many amenities, including shopping centers, healthcare facilities, and international schools, making it an attractive option for families.

Famagusta (Ayia Napa and Protaras)

The Famagusta region, including the popular resort towns of Ayia Napa and Protaras, is located on the eastern coast of Cyprus. This area is known for its stunning beaches, crystal-clear waters, and vibrant nightlife. Ayia Napa, in particular, is famous for its lively party scene, attracting a younger crowd during the summer months.

Aerial view of the bay of Protaras

However, Protaras offers a more family-friendly environment, with quieter beaches and a range of recreational activities. The Famagusta region is ideal for those who enjoy an active lifestyle, with plenty of opportunities for water sports, hiking, and outdoor adventures.

BANKING

Banking in Cyprus is straightforward and modern, with a wide range of services available to expatriates. The Cypriot banking system is well-regulated and operates in accordance with European Union standards. Major international banks, as well as reputable local banks, operate across the island, providing services in multiple languages, including English.

Bank of Cyprus Branch

Opening a bank account in Cyprus is a relatively simple process, especially for expatriates. Most banks offer accounts in multiple currencies, including Euros, US Dollars, and British Pounds, which is convenient for those dealing with international transactions. To open a bank account, you will generally need to provide the following documents:

- Passport or national identity card
- Proof of address (such as a utility bill or rental agreement)
- Proof of income or employment (such as a work contract or bank statement)

Some banks may also require a reference from your previous bank or a local reference. The process typically takes a few days, and once your account is opened, you will have access to a wide range of banking services, including online and mobile banking, credit and debit cards, and international transfers.

BENEFITS OF MOVING TO CYPRUS

One of the most compelling reasons to move to Cyprus is the significant improvement in the quality of life that expatriates often experience. Cyprus offers a laid-back lifestyle that is ideally suited to those who wish to escape the fast-paced and frequently stressful environment of larger cities in other parts of Europe or the world. The island's pace of life is slower, with a strong emphasis on work-life balance, making it easier to enjoy leisure time and focus on personal well-being.

The cost of living in Cyprus is relatively low compared to many Western European countries, particularly in terms of housing, groceries, and utilities. This affordability allows expatriates to enjoy a higher standard of living, with access to comfortable housing, quality healthcare, and other essential services without the financial strain that might be felt elsewhere. Additionally, the island's crime rate is low, contributing to a sense of safety and security for residents.

Healthcare in Cyprus is of a high standard, with both public and private healthcare systems offering comprehensive medical services. The public healthcare system is accessible to residents, including expatriates, who contribute to the social insurance scheme. In contrast, private healthcare provides additional options for those seeking faster service or more specialized care. The availability of English-speaking medical professionals further enhances the appeal of Cyprus for expatriates.

Education is another important aspect of life for expatriates, particularly those with families. Cyprus boasts a range of international schools that cater to various educational systems, including the British curriculum, the International Baccalaureate (IB), and other European curricula. These schools provide high-quality education in English and other languages, ensuring that expatriate children can continue their studies in a familiar educational environment.

More Sunny Days

Cyprus is renowned for its Mediterranean climate, which is one of the sunniest in Europe. The island enjoys more than 300 days of sunshine each year, with warm temperatures throughout most of the year. This sunny climate contributes to a better mood and overall well-being and encourages an outdoor lifestyle that is difficult to achieve in colder, cloudier regions.

The pristine Akamas peninsula, southwestern Cyprus

The long, hot summers and mild winters in Cyprus allow for year-round outdoor activities, including swimming, hiking, cycling, and dining al fresco. The consistent sunshine makes it easy for residents to maintain an active lifestyle, which is further supported by the island's beautiful natural environment. Whether it's spending a day at the beach, exploring the Troodos Mountains, or enjoying a leisurely walk along the coastal paths, the sunny weather enhances the enjoyment of these activities.

Living Near the Beach

One of Cyprus's most attractive aspects of life is the proximity to some of the most stunning beaches in the Mediterranean. The island's coastline stretches for miles, offering diverse beaches, from golden sandy shores to secluded rocky coves. Living near the beach is a reality for many expatriates in Cyprus, where coastal towns and cities like Limassol, Paphos, and Larnaca offer a blend of modern amenities and easy access to the sea.

For those who love the beach, Cyprus provides endless opportunities to enjoy the sea and sun. Whether it's swimming in the crystal-clear waters, sunbathing on the soft sands, or engaging in water sports like windsurfing, scuba diving, and sailing, the beaches of Cyprus offer something for everyone. The island's beaches are also known for their cleanliness and safety, with many of them being awarded Blue Flag status, a testament to their environmental quality and amenities.

An International Ambience

Cyprus has a long history of being a crossroads between cultures, and this is reflected in its diverse and international atmosphere. The island is home to a large expatriate community, with residents from the UK, Russia, Greece, and other European countries, as well as from farther afield. This international presence is particularly strong in cities like Limassol, Nicosia, and Paphos, where expatriates from all over the world live, work, and socialize.

The international ambiance in Cyprus is evident in many aspects of daily life. English is widely spoken, particularly in business, education, and tourism, making it easy for expatriates to communicate and integrate into the local community. Road signs and directions are usually written in dual languages (Greek and English). International schools, multinational companies, and global events contribute to the island's cosmopolitan feel.

For expatriates, this international environment offers numerous opportunities to connect with people from different backgrounds and cultures. Many expatriates find it easy to build social networks and form friendships with both locals and fellow expatriates. International clubs, associations, and social groups further enhance this sense of community, providing avenues for socializing, networking, and engaging in cultural activities.

Cultural diversity in Cyprus is also reflected in the island's cuisine, festivals, and arts scene. Expatriates can enjoy a wide range of culinary experiences, from traditional Cypriot dishes to international cuisine, often within the same neighborhood. The island's cultural calendar is filled with events celebrating local traditions and international influences, allowing expatriates to experience a rich tapestry of cultural experiences.

Furthermore, Cyprus's strategic location in the Eastern Mediterranean makes it an ideal base for exploring other regional countries. The island's proximity to Europe, Asia, and Africa means that expatriates can easily travel to nearby destinations for business or leisure. This accessibility enhances the international lifestyle that many expatriates seek, allowing them to experience different cultures and broaden their horizons.

HEALTH CARE

Public healthcare in Cyprus is available to all residents who contribute to the social insurance system. This includes expatriates who are employed or self-employed in Cyprus. Public healthcare services are generally free or provided at a low cost, and they cover a wide range of medical treatments, including general practitioner visits, specialist consultations, hospital care, and emergency services.

Public hospitals and clinics are located throughout the island, and well-trained medical professionals staff them. However, waiting times for non-emergency treatments can be longer in the public sector compared to private healthcare.

Private Healthcare

Expatriates moving to Cyprus should consider taking out health insurance to cover the cost of private health care. Several options are available, ranging from local health insurance plans to international policies offering coverage in Cyprus and abroad.

Private health care offers faster access to treatment, more personalized care, and a wider choice of medical facilities and specialists. Private health care is widely available throughout the island, with numerous hospitals, clinics, and private medical centers offering a full range of services.

INTERNET SPEED

Internet services in Cyprus are widely available, extending to urban and rural areas. Cyprus's main internet service providers offer a range of packages, including broadband, fiber optic, and mobile internet services. Fiber optic connections are becoming increasingly common, particularly in cities like Nicosia, Limassol, Paphos, and Larnaca, providing high-speed internet access to residents.

Internet speeds in Cyprus are generally reliable and sufficient for most online activities, including streaming, video conferencing, and online gaming. Average download speeds for fixed broadband connections typically range from 50 Mbps to 100 Mbps, depending on the service provider and the type of connection. Fiber optic connections can offer even higher speeds, reaching up to 1 Gbps in some areas.

Mobile Internet

Mobile internet is also widely accessible across Cyprus, with 4G coverage available in most areas. Major mobile network providers offer competitive data plans, making staying connected while on the go easy. The rollout of 5G networks is underway, promising even faster mobile internet speeds in the near future.

LIFESTYLE

Cyprus offers a relaxed and enjoyable lifestyle, making it a popular destination for expatriates from around the world. The island's Mediterranean climate, diverse culture, and outdoor-oriented lifestyle contribute to its appeal.

Outdoor Activities

Cyprus's warm climate and beautiful landscapes are ideal for outdoor activities. The island offers a variety of recreational opportunities, including hiking in the Troodos Mountains, cycling along scenic coastal routes, and exploring nature reserves. Water sports such as sailing, diving, and snorkeling are also popular, particularly in the coastal areas of Limassol, Larnaca, and Paphos.

Sea walk in Limassol

Cyprus is home to numerous beaches, many of which have been awarded Blue Flag status for their cleanliness and safety. The island's beaches vary from lively tourist spots with plenty of amenities to more secluded and quiet locations, catering to different preferences.

Cuisine and Dining

Cypriot cuisine is a delicious blend of Mediterranean and Middle Eastern flavors, featuring fresh ingredients such as olive oil, herbs, vegetables, and seafood. Traditional dishes include meze (a selection of small dishes), souvlaki (grilled meat skewers), and halloumi cheese, which is a Cypriot specialty.

Dining out is a significant part of social life in Cyprus, and the island offers a wide range of restaurants, from local tavernas serving traditional Cypriot food to international eateries offering cuisine from around the world. The cost of dining out is generally affordable, making it easy for expatriates to enjoy the local food culture.

Social Life and Community

Cyprus has a vibrant expatriate community, particularly in cities like Limassol, Nicosia, and Paphos. This community is supported by various social clubs, organizations, and events that provide opportunities for networking, making friends, and integrating into local life.

Socializing in Cyprus often revolves around outdoor activities, dining, and cultural events. The island hosts numerous festivals throughout the year, celebrating everything from music and arts to wine and traditional Cypriot culture. These events allow expatriates to experience the local culture and connect with locals and other expatriates.

IMMIGRATION AND RESIDENCY

Cyprus offers a range of immigration and residency options for expatriates, making it relatively straightforward for foreign nationals to live and work on the island.

EU/EEA Citizens

Citizens of European Union (EU) and European Economic Area (EEA) countries have the right to live and work in Cyprus without the need for a visa or work permit. However, EU/EEA nationals who intend to stay in Cyprus for over three months must register with the local immigration authorities and obtain a Registration Certificate, commonly known as a "Yellow Slip." This document confirms their legal right to reside in Cyprus and is necessary for accessing various services, such as healthcare and opening a bank account.

To apply for a Yellow Slip, EU/EEA nationals need to provide proof of employment or sufficient financial resources, as well as proof of address in Cyprus.

Non-EU/EEA Citizens

Non-EU/EEA citizens who wish to move to Cyprus for work, study, or other purposes must apply for a relevant visa and/or residency permit before entering the country. The type of visa required depends on the purpose of the stay, such as a work visa, student visa, or family reunification visa.

Once in Cyprus, non-EU/EEA nationals can apply for a Temporary Residence Permit (commonly known as a "Pink Slip"), which allows them to stay in Cyprus for an extended period. Temporary Residence Permits are usually valid for one year and can be renewed annually.

For those who intend to stay in Cyprus long-term, there are several options for obtaining Permanent Residency. The most common routes to Permanent Residency include:

- **Investment Program**: Cyprus offers a Permanent Residency by Investment program, which allows non-EU/EEA citizens to obtain permanent residency by making a qualifying investment in the country, such as purchasing property or investing in a business.
- **Long-Term Residency**: Non-EU/EEA nationals who have legally resided in Cyprus for at least five years may apply for Long-Term Residency status, which grants them the right to reside in Cyprus indefinitely.

AFTERWORD

As an online business professional, your ability to work from anywhere offers unparalleled freedom. But with that freedom comes the responsibility to make strategic decisions that maximize your financial potential. If you're seeking a tax-efficient environment that supports your business and enhances your quality of life, Cyprus is the destination you've been searching for.

Imagine keeping more of what you earn. Cyprus offers one of Europe's most favorable tax regimes, particularly for digital nomads and online entrepreneurs. With a flat corporate tax rate of just 12.5%, among the lowest in the EU, and a non-domicile regime that exempts foreign-sourced income like dividends and interest from taxation, Cyprus allows you to reduce your tax liabilities significantly. This means more money in your pocket to reinvest in your business or enjoy the finer things in life.

Benefit from a strategic location and robust infrastructure. Cyprus is ideally situated at the crossroads of Europe, Asia, and Africa, offering easy access to key markets. The country also has a well-developed digital infrastructure, ensuring you can run your online business seamlessly. Whether you're managing a global e-commerce platform, offering freelance services, or operating a tech startup, Cyprus provides the connectivity and stability you need to thrive.

Enjoy a superior quality of life. Beyond the financial advantages, Cyprus offers a high standard of living with its stunning Mediterranean climate, beautiful landscapes, and vibrant culture. Whether relaxing on the beach after a productive day or exploring the island's rich history on weekends, Cyprus provides the perfect backdrop for both work and leisure. Plus, with a low cost of living compared to other EU countries, you'll find that your income goes further, enhancing your overall lifestyle.

Join a thriving community of entrepreneurs. Cyprus has become a magnet for digital nomads, entrepreneurs, and innovators worldwide. By relocating, you'll join a dynamic community of like-minded professionals, opening doors to new collaborations, partnerships, and growth opportunities.

Simplify your tax planning and compliance. Cyprus's transparent and straightforward tax system makes staying compliant while maximizing your savings easy. With access to experienced local tax advisors and a government committed to maintaining a business-friendly environment, you can focus on what you do best—growing your online business—while resting assured that your tax affairs are in good hands.

In today's global economy, where your business is based can make all the difference to your bottom line. By moving to Cyprus, you're not just moving to a new country—you're making a strategic decision to enhance your financial future, expand your business horizons, and enjoy a quality of life that is second to none. Make the smart move today. Discover the tax benefits, vibrant community, and unparalleled lifestyle that await you in Cyprus. It's time to take your online business to the next level—where your hard work translates into real savings and a richer life.

SUGGESTED REFERENCES

Suggested References for Further Study

1. **OECD - Base Erosion and Profit Shifting (BEPS) Initiative**

- The OECD's BEPS initiative provides comprehensive insights into the global efforts to combat tax avoidance strategies that exploit gaps and mismatches in tax rules.
- URL: https://www.oecd.org/tax/beps/

1. **"International Taxation: Principles and Practices" by Lynne Oats**

- This book offers a detailed examination of international tax principles, including discussions on tax treaties, transfer pricing, and the impact of global tax reforms.
- ISBN: 9781352006019

1. **Cyprus Tax Department – Official Website**

- The Cyprus Tax Department's official site provides up-to-date information on tax regulations, application procedures, and guidelines for both individuals and corporations.
- URL: http://www.mof.gov.cy/mof/tax/taxdep.nsf/index_en/index_en?OpenDocument

1. **"Cyprus International Trusts: Law and Practice" by Christiana Serghides**

- This book offers an in-depth analysis of Cyprus International Trusts, including their legal and tax implications, making it a valuable resource for those interested in asset protection and tax planning.
- ISBN: 9780414032075

1. **"The Non-Dom Regime: A Practical Guide" by James Quarmby and Jonathan Schwarz**

- This guide provides a practical overview of non-dom regimes in various jurisdictions, including Cyprus, with detailed discussions on tax planning strategies and compliance.
- ISBN: 9781787421427

1. **The International Tax Planning Association (ITPA) - Resources and Publications**

- ITPA provides a wide range of resources, articles, and publications on international tax planning, including specific focus areas like the non-dom regime and tax treaties.
- URL: https://www.itpa.org/

1. **"Taxation in the European Union" by E. Philip Davis and Benny Geys**

- This academic book explores taxation within the EU, offering perspectives on tax harmonization, competition, and the impact of EU regulations on member states like Cyprus.
- ISBN: 9781788972195

1. **Cyprus Investment Promotion Agency (Invest Cyprus) - Publications**

- Invest Cyprus provides a wealth of information on the benefits of relocating to Cyprus, including detailed guides on the tax incentives and business environment.
- URL: https://www.investcyprus.org.cy/

1. **"Global Tax Fairness" edited by Thomas Pogge and Krishen Mehta**

- This collection of essays delves into the ethical and policy dimensions of global tax fairness, including the role of tax havens and international tax competition.
- ISBN: 9780198725343

1. **PubMed – Research Articles on International Taxation**

- PubMed offers a database of academic journals and articles related to international taxation, policy impacts, and economic studies. Relevant articles can be found using keywords like "international taxation," "tax planning," and "non-domicile regimes."
- URL: https://pubmed.ncbi.nlm.nih.gov/

1. **"Double Taxation Treaties: A Critical Analysis" by Philip Baker**

- This book provides an in-depth critique and analysis of double taxation treaties, essential for understanding their impact on cross-border tax planning and compliance.
- ISBN: 9781904501771

1. **International Monetary Fund (IMF) - Reports on Tax Policy and Administration**

- The IMF publishes reports and working papers on global tax policy, with insights into the taxation systems of various countries, including Cyprus.
- URL: https://www.imf.org/en/Publications/WP

www.ingramcontent.com/pod-product-compliance
Lightning Source LLC
Chambersburg PA
CBHW070400230526
45471CB00006B/2652